FIVE-MINUTE WARMUPS

FOR THE MIDDLE GRADES

Quick-and-Easy Activities
To Reinforce Basic Skills

by Bea Green, Sandi Schlichting, and Mary Ellen Thomas

Incentive Publications, Inc.
Nashville, Tennessee

Cover by Marta Drayton and Joe Shibley
Edited by Jan Keeling and Leslie Britt

ISBN 0-86530-263-4

PRINTED IN THE UNITED STATES OF AMERICA

Table of Contents

LANGUAGE ARTS

MATH

SOCIAL STUDIES

BONUS: SELF-AWARENESS ACTIVITIES

PREFACE

How many times have you realized that you have just five or ten minutes left before it's time for your middle graders to go to lunch, to the media center, or to P.E. class? Or perhaps you've just finished a terrific language lesson and find that there are five minutes to go before the social studies teacher is ready to change classes.

It may not be possible to eliminate those extra five-minute periods even with the best of planning; however, five minutes a day adds up to over fifteen hours of instructional time in a school year. We believe those odd extra moments can be put to excellent use with little or no preparation at all. *Five-Minute Warmups for the Middle Grades* provides the key to using lag times for effective reinforcement of language arts, math, and social studies skills and concepts.

These warmups are more than just ways to fill in odd moments. You will find that they spark enthusiasm in your students, "warming them up" for the next activity at hand. Many of the activities can be used as great lead-ins for new units. Others are meant for drill or for review of basic skills and facts. Some are simply fun-filled ways to put skills and knowledge to work. You will find that many of the activities can be extended into full-length lessons.

At the back of the book is a bonus section of self-awareness activities. The wise middle grades teacher knows when the atmosphere of trust in a classroom has reached a level where such activities can be of benefit. Though there may be a bit of initial reluctance, these are the activities that are most likely to engage the students and that they are most likely to want to extend beyond a five-minute time period.

Happy Teaching!

Language

Language

Language

Language

Language

Language

Language

Language

Language

Language

BEGINNINGS AND ENDINGS

To practice using prefixes and suffixes, give students one of the examples below. Ask them to name words containing that prefix or suffix. When they run out of examples, go to another.

Prefixes

pre-	de-	pro-	ex-
con-	re-	un-	

Suffixes

-able	-ing	-al	-ness
-ly	-ed	-er	

WHO'S WHO

Review with your class the meaning of the suffix "-ist" and then call out the following occupations. Ask your students to tell what each person would study. If they don't know the answer, tell them. Repeat the activity frequently and watch them learn!

ichthyologist	fish	audiologist	hearing
anthropologist	man	hydrologist	water
economist	money	podiatrist	feet
agronomist	soil	pharmacist	drugs
zoologist	animals	entomologist	insects
botanist	plants	etymologist	words

MAD SCRAMBLE

Write one or two of your class's current spelling words on the board. Ask students to scramble the letters to make new words. They may use all or only some of the letters. Give them three or four minutes to work. Then ask one student to read his or her list. As the list is read aloud, other students with the same words should cross them off their lists. Students may score one point for each word they made that wasn't read from the first list.

A variation:
Select one spelling word. Do not write it on the board. Instead, write two or three words that could also be made with those letters. See if students can decide which spelling word you selected.

MAKE IT MORE

Students in all grades need constant review and practice in making singular words plural.

Give students singular words and ask them to pronounce and spell their plural forms. You may also ask students to name the rule being followed in making the plural. (Save irregular plurals for a separate drill.)

Some words to start with:

valley	city	box
knife	day	shelf
story	book	boy
dish	half	monkey
penny	dime	key
bubble	bench	pencil

TWO BY TWO

Have students practice thinking of things that come in twos or pairs. Ask each student to name something that is found or bought two-at-a-time. (Some things are a single item but are called a pair.)

Examples:

a pair of pajamas	socks	eyes
a pair of earrings	scissors	ears
arms	twins	jeans
legs	lollipops	long johns
shoes	handcuffs	glasses

SNAP IT!

Call out one of the words listed below. Ask students to "snap out" another word that can be combined with your word to make a compound word. Students should provide as many combinations as possible before going on to the next word.

class	line	eye	yard	board
read	shake	out	lid	book
camp	in	side	out	man
hand	junk	some	boy	foot
door	week	end	time	
day	every	room	air	

GOOD WORDS, BAD WORDS

Sometimes two words mean almost the same thing, but elicit different feelings when they are used.

Read each word pair listed below and let students decide which word is more likely to cause bad feelings.

cheap / inexpensive	dumb / ignorant
thin / skinny	thrifty / cheap
chubby / fat	nosy / curious
sly / sneaky	enthusiastic / rowdy
clever / tricky	timid / shy

ABC WORD GAMES

Choose a category from this list. Have students think of words in that category that start with each of the letters of the alphabet. Call on the first student to give an appropriate word that starts with "A" and then continue around the class. Any student who cannot think of a word for his or her turn may be skipped. Come back to those students after each student has had a chance to answer or on the next round.

Sample
categories:

proper nouns	compound words
common nouns	hyphenated words
adjectives	five-letter words
adverbs	words that mean "said"

PRO OR CON?

Ask one of the questions listed below. Select one student to speak for the idea and one student to speak against the idea. Give each student about one minute to speak. Then ask the rest of the class which side they agree with (by a show of hands).

✦ **From now on, trees should not be cut down.**

✦ **Each person should drive as fast or as slowly as he or she thinks is safe.**

✦ **Families should be allowed to have a limited number of appliances that require electricity.**

✦ **Girls should be allowed to do all of the same things that boys do.**

✦ **Medical care should be offered free of charge to everyone in this country.**

ATTENTION: ACROSTICS

Print a word on the board vertically. You may choose from the list of "substantial" words given below or provide your own.

Liberty   Achievement   Friendship   Conservation

Instruct students to write an acrostic poem by writing one sentence that starts with each letter of the word.

Example:

Liberty means accepting responsibility.
I am proud of my country.
Betsy Ross designed the flag.
Everyone is created equal.
Red in the flag means courage.
The liberty bell is located in Philadelphia.
You should show respect for our flag.

AD-WISE

Let students try their hands at advertising. Name one of the following items. Let students give as many brief advertising ideas as they can in five minutes for that item.

- ✦ **polka dot socks**
- ✦ **spicy toothpaste**
- ✦ **bubblegum-scented hairspray**
- ✦ **calendars without Mondays**
- ✦ **shoes that expand as your feet grow**
- ✦ **pocket-sized vacuum cleaners**
- ✦ **invisible eyeglasses**

THINK ON YOUR FEET

Impromptu speaking gives students a chance to think on their feet. Select one of the subjects below. Call on one student to talk about the subject for about one minute. Select a different subject for the next student. Add other subjects to the list for future talks.

Suggested Subjects:
- ✦ **You are the basketball hoop in the school gymnasium. Describe your day.**
- ✦ **You are the principal of your school for today. What will you do?**
- ✦ **You are an Arctic tern making an amazing migration from the Arctic to the Antarctic. Tell about your trip.**
- ✦ **You will make all decisions about the school lunch menu. Tell us about your decisions.**

STORY CHAIN

List one of the following word banks on the board. Explain that the class is going to compose a story together (orally). Each person will contribute just one sentence. Students use the word bank to help them compose the story. Remind the last people in the room that they will be responsible for bringing the story to an end. If a student seems "stuck" when it is his or her turn, come back to him or her later.

Word Banks	#1	#2	#3	#4
	airplane	house	flowers	power failure
	blizzard	fun	bees	party
	hungry	fire	gift	emergency
	bear	stairs	race	panic
	trouble	twins	bouquet	hero
	crash	trapped	scream	friends

DECISIONS, DECISIONS

Let as many students as possible respond to the following situations:

You have just received $100 to spend on anything you want. How would your choice be affected if:

✦ **you had to spend it within the next hour?**

✦ **you couldn't spend it all in one place?**

✦ **you had to first keep it for three months?**

✦ **you had to spend it on something that would last at least five years?**

✦ **you had to spend it on something that wouldn't last more than a day?**

✦ **you had to spend it on someone else?**

FORWARDS, BACKWARDS

Palindromes are words that read the same backwards as they do forwards. Give your students a few examples.

pop
mom
anna
wow

Have your students list as many palindromes as possible while you record them on the board.

PROPERLY SPEAKING

To reinforce the difference between common and proper nouns, give students a common noun and ask them to name a proper noun in that category. (You may sometimes want to give proper nouns and let the students name the appropriate common noun.)

Sample common nouns:

movie	TV show	place
book	street	park
city	woman	holiday
man	state	president
month	day	river

SISTERS AND BROTHERS

Ask the students:

✦ **How many of you have younger sisters or brothers?**
✦ **What are some of the problems of being the older sister or brother?**
✦ **What are some of the advantages of being the older sister or brother?**

Ask the students who have older sisters and brothers to discuss some of the advantages and disadvantages of being younger siblings.

Let any of the students who are an only child tell what that is like.

SLIMMING SUBJECTS

Students often find it difficult to begin writing a story or report because their topics are too broad.

Give students one of the broad topics listed below and ask them to suggest related topics that are more narrow.

Topics:

mammals	**famous authors**
airplanes	**travel**
basketball	**tennis**
music	**painting**
North America	**trees**
dogs	**Africa**

PLASTIC MONEY

Most young adults are familiar with the use of credit cards, but they may not be aware of the advantages and disadvantages of using plastic money. Lead a discussion of the good and bad aspects of using credit cards.

GOOD
- ✦ don't have to carry cash
- ✦ helpful in emergencies
- ✦ can buy now, pay later
- ✦ good identification
- ✦ helps you take advantage of unexpected good sales

BAD
- ✦ spend more than you make
- ✦ cards can be stolen and misused
- ✦ tempts you into impulsive buying
- ✦ makes spending too easy
- ✦ may ruin your credit if abused

Math

Math

Math

Math

Math

Math

Math

Math

Math

Math

PLACES, PLEASE!

Give students an opportunity to practice place value identification. Write one of the following numbers on the board. Ask students to name the value of a particular digit in that number. Select numbers based on the ability level of your students.

Whole Numbers 3<u>4</u>56 103,10<u>3</u>
12,<u>3</u>78 9<u>9</u>9

Decimal Numbers 1<u>2</u>.342 99.99<u>9</u>
.5<u>6</u>02 103.<u>1</u>03

Make up other numbers as you repeat the activity.

NUMBER LINE-UP

Have each student jot down a two- or three-digit number on a sheet of paper. The numbers should be large enough for the entire class to see.

Ask students to stand up and display their numbers if they meet certain conditions you will now announce. Choose from the following ideas or make up your own conditions.

✦ **a number under 100**

✦ **a number that is a multiple of 5 (or 3, 6, etc.)**

✦ **a number with digits that total to a certain sum**

✦ **a number with digits that are in order from largest to smallest (765, etc.)**

✦ **a number with digits that are all even numbers (244, 468, etc.)**

METRIC MADNESS

After students have learned metric measurement, try this activity for practice. You will need to list the units on the board in order from smallest to largest:

    millimeter   centimeter   decimeter   meter   kilometer

Then ask students to decide if you would have to multiply or divide in order to change from:

✦ **millimeters to centimeters (divide by 10)**

✦ **kilometers to meters (multiply by 1000)**

✦ **centimeters to decimeters (divide by 10)**

✦ **decimeters to meters (divide by 10)**

✦ **meters to centimeters (multiply by 100)**

✦ **meters to kilometers (divide by 1000)**

SIZE IT UP

This is a good measurement activity for a restless class. Give each student a ruler and ask them to find something in the classroom that is:

✦ **exactly one foot long**

✦ **less than six inches long**

✦ **two inches thick**

✦ **more than five inches wide**

✦ **half an inch wide**

Students can practice their metric measurement skills by measuring objects in centimeters, millimeters, and decimeters.

OPERATIONS

Give students the examples below and ask them to tell you what operations must be used to arrive at the answers:

1) I start with 24 and end up with 27. (addition)
2) I start with 100 and end up with 10. (division by 10 or subtraction of 90)
3) I start with 144 and end up with 140. (subtraction)
4) I start with 3 and end up with 33. (addition of 30 or multiplication by 11)

Add other examples to the list or let students challenge each other with original examples. (The student thinking up the example gets just as much practice.)

SIDE BY SIDE

Can your students name multi-sided closed figures?

Try these to find out:
+ **three-sided figure (triangle)**
+ **four-sided figures (quadrilateral, rectangle, square, rhombus, parallelogram, trapezoid)**
+ **five-sided figure (pentagon)**
+ **six-sided figure (hexagon)**
+ **seven-sided figure (heptagon)**
+ **eight-sided figure (octagon)**
+ **nine-sided figure (nonagon)**
+ **ten-sided figure (decagon)**
+ **twelve-sided figure (dodecagon)**

PRESIDENT'S MONEY

Can your students tell you which president's portrait is on each denomination of currency? Let them try to name them all.

$1.00	**Washington**
$5.00	**Lincoln**
$10.00	**Hamilton**
$20.00	**Jackson**
$50.00	**Grant**
$100.00	**Franklin**

Once students have learned which faces are on each denomination of currency, ask questions such as, "How much money do I have if I have one Washington and one Lincoln?" and "How much money do I have if I have one Franklin, two Grants, and a Jackson?"

RACE TO 25

Students form two teams. The first member of Team A goes to the board and writes either "1" or "1" and "2." The first student from Team B goes to the board next and writes the next consecutive number or the next two consecutive numbers. The teams continue to alternate sending members to the board to write one or two consecutive numbers. The team whose member writes the number "25" on the board is the winner.

After you have completed this activity several times, ask students what strategies they are using. Does it seem to make a difference if both teams employ the same strategy? Can you control the results better by being the first team to play? Would the game be easier or harder if you could write three consecutive numbers?

MOVING ON

Play this game to let students practice multiplication facts. Select one student to begin. That student should stand up next to the first student in the first row. Call out or display a flash card with a multiplication problem on it. The first of the two students to answer correctly gets to move on to the next student's desk. (If the seated student answers first, he or she trades places with the standing student.)

The student standing continues to move around the room as long as he or she answers correctly first. Any student who makes it back to his or her original starting position can be declared the winner!

TRICKY NUMBERS

Tell students to follow your directions and you will guess the numbers they start with:

1. **Write down your favorite number.**
2. **Multiply the number by 4.**
3. **Add 20 to the product.**
4. **Divide the answer by 4.**

To find a student's mystery number, ask what the final answer was. Subtract five from this number. The result is the student's starting number.

After you have impressed them with your ESP, do a few examples on the board and trace the "magic" of the trick.

NAME A UNIT

Name one of the following objects or actions and have students name the appropriate unit for measuring it:

✦ **time it takes to run six feet (seconds)**

✦ **bolts of fabric or ribbon (yards)**

✦ **width of a chocolate chip (millimeters or 16ths of an inch)**

✦ **amount of milk in a glass (ounces or milliliters)**

✦ **swinging of a pendulum (times per minute . . . a relationship as well as a unit is needed)**

✦ **distance between two cities (kilometers or miles)**

✦ **length of a pencil (inches or centimeters)**

✦ **area of a floor (square feet or square yards)**

RELATED NUMBERS

Write several pairs of numbers on the board. Ask students to tell how all the pairs of numbers are alike or what relationship they share.

Examples:

✦ 6, 36   10, 100   15, 225
   (Each pair is the square root of a number and that number.)

✦ 13, 19   55, 61   117, 123
   (Six has been added to the first number of each pair.)

✦ 2, 18   3, 12   6, 6
   (The numbers of each pair are factors of 36.)

✦ 2, 12   9, 99   3, 27
   (The second number of each pair is a multiple of the first number.)

EVEN STEVEN

Some things are not as easy to share "Even Steven" as other things. For instance, it's not as easy to share a bicycle as it is to share two quarters with another person. Ask your students to tell how they would share these things:

- ✦ Four people must share a sandwich.
- ✦ You have rented a bicycle built-for-two for an hour. There are five of you paying for the bike. How do you share the bike?
- ✦ There are twelve new boxes of crayons, but thirty-six students in your class. How will your teacher have you share the crayons?
- ✦ There are nine people in your reading group, but the play has only six characters. What will you do?

EQUAL VALUES

Ask your students what would be an equal amount of money to:

- ✦ 3 quarters (7 dimes plus 1 nickel or 75 pennies)
- ✦ 2 dollars (20 dimes or 40 nickels or 4 half-dollars)
- ✦ 10 nickels (5 dimes or 50 pennies or 2 quarters)
- ✦ 3 half-dollars (6 quarters or 15 dimes or 1 dollar and 2 quarters)
- ✦ 2 quarters, 1 dime, and 1 nickel (65 pennies or 13 nickels or 4 dimes, 4 nickels, and 5 pennies)

Make up other examples for students to practice money values.

ADD ON

Separate the class into two teams. List the numbers 1-10 on the board. Choose a target number between 15 and 55. Let one member of the first team come to the board and select one of the listed numbers. Cross that number off of the list and write it on the board in another spot. Then let one member of the second team come to the board and cross out another number from the list. Add that amount to the first number that was selected. Continue to let members of each team come to the board, select a number from those remaining, and add it to the others. The team whose member hits a target number wins.

Example with a target of 23:
- ✦ "Team A" chooses 3. "Team B" chooses 7. The total is 10.
- ✦ "Team A" chooses 8. Total is 18. "Team B" chooses 5.
- ✦ The total is now 23, the target number. "Team B" wins.

DIGITS

Ask students to write a two-digit number in which:
- ✦ **The sum of the digits is 12 (or any other amount).**
- ✦ **The first digit is larger than the second.**
- ✦ **There is a difference of 6 between the two digits.**
- ✦ **One digit is the double of the other.**

Ask students to write three-digit numbers in which:
- ✦ **All three digits are even (or odd).**
- ✦ **The number reads the same forwards and backwards.**
- ✦ **The digits total a specific amount.**
- ✦ **All of the digits are different and are written in a specified order (from largest to smallest or vice versa).**

Try other activities with four- and five-digit numbers.

TALKING MATH

These sayings sound like they are about math or numbers. What do your students think? Ask them to explain the meanings of the following expressions:

- ✦ **Hang ten.**
- ✦ **Count me in.**
- ✦ **six of one, half dozen of the other**
- ✦ **It doesn't add up.**
- ✦ **cheaper by the dozen**
- ✦ **Take five.**
- ✦ **double or nothing**
- ✦ **one for the money, two for the show**

DATED DIGITS

Have the students write their birth dates in digit form. Example: July 7, 1982, written in digit form, is 7/7/82.

Try some of these other activities using digit dates. Give students the date of a holiday in digit form. Who can decipher the holiday first? Or, give the holiday or special date and let students practice writing it as a set of digits.

Examples:

Christmas	**12/25/94 (Any year may be specified.)**
Valentine's Day	**2/14/94**
Halloween	**10/31/94**

ON THE JOB

Brainstorm in small groups or as an entire class to see how many math-related jobs or careers your students can think of in five minutes.

As a variation, think of careers that use specific math skills, such as:

✦ **counting money**
✦ **recording elapsed time**
✦ **estimating**
✦ **measuring**
✦ **tallying**

SYMMETRY SEARCH

Have a symmetry search in your classroom. Ask students to find things in the room that have lines of symmetry.

As they identify objects with lines of symmetry, ask how many lines of symmetry each object has. Some objects have rotational symmetry (the object can be rotated and still have lines of symmetry in each position).

If you have access to small hand mirrors, let students examine the letters of the alphabet as they write them on the board or on paper. Do the letters look the same when reflected in the mirrors? Is the symmetry horizontal or vertical? Which letters have no lines of symmetry?

STORY FACTS

Students are used to finding answers, not problems! Give students a set of facts and let them come up with a problem suitable for those facts.

Example:
Two times four equals eight. (Fact)
John bought two boxes of candy bars. Each box had four bars in it.
How many candy bars did John have? (Problem)

Other facts:
100 - 87 = 13
86 ÷ 2 = 43
27 + 36 = 63

Let students challenge each other with facts without problems.

WHAT'S WRONG?

Write some problems on the board that have intentional errors in them. Forget to carry when you add, forget to change digits when you borrow, don't carry the correct digit when you add a column that totals to more than nine, and so on.

Challenge students to find your errors. Ask them to tell you how the problems would be solved to arrive at the correct answers.

Or, write five problems and answers on the board. Let students find the one problem that is wrong and tell what is wrong with it.

To be aware of common errors is helpful to students when proofing their own work.

BODY MATH

Let your students experience "Body Math." Have them use the width of their palms, the length of their feet, or the length of their pinky fingers as a standard unit by which to measure the:

- ✦ **width of the room,**
- ✦ **height of a chair,**
- ✦ **distance between desks, or**
- ✦ **any other distances in your classroom.**

Discuss the results and how standardized units are necessary in order to accurately communicate measurements to others.

TIME SENSE

This activity will help students develop a better sense of short periods of time.

Have students put their heads on their desks and close their eyes. Name a specific amount of time that you want them to wait (10 seconds, 45 seconds, 1 minute, 2 minutes, etc.). Instruct students to raise their hands when they think the specified amount of time has elapsed. Say "start" and begin timing silently.

When you repeat this exercise for the same amount of time several times, your students will begin to more accurately estimate the measured passage of time.

MENTAL MATH

Have students practice mental math skills and estimation at the same time. Explain that you will call out two numbers, one at a time. As you call out each number, the class (or an individual student), should respond with that number rounded to the nearest tens place. After you have called out both numbers, the class or student should respond with the estimated total or difference, whichever you specify.

Example:

Teacher, "23."	**Student, "20."**
Teacher, "47."	**Student, "50."**
Teacher, "Total?"	**Student, "70."**

You can then add or subtract the actual numbers on the board to see how close the estimation is to the actual sum or difference.

YOUR OPINION COUNTS

Let your students discuss the following questions:
- ✦ **How are the numbers 50 and 500 alike? How are they different?**
- ✦ **What is your favorite two-digit number? Why is it your favorite?**
- ✦ **Do you have a lucky number? What is it? Why do you think that it is lucky for you?**
- ✦ **Are some multiplication facts more difficult to learn than others? Which ones? Are some easier?**
- ✦ **Is it more difficult to learn to regroup in subtraction or in addition?**
- ✦ **What is your favorite math activity?**

MATH WORD CHALLENGE

Challenge students to know their math vocabulary. Call out one of the words listed below and ask for a volunteer to explain its meaning. Any student who disagrees can challenge the definition and correct it.

vertex	factor	quadrilateral
perimeter	product	multiple
area	quotient	prime number
fraction	sum	composite number
equivalent	divisor	circumference
numerator	ray	diameter
denominator	line	square

See additional math terms on the Math Terms card below.

MATH TERMS

Challenge students further with these math terms (including some computer lingo):

binary	absolute value	closed figure
byte	addend	Cartesian set
RAM	axis	cardinal number
decagon	cube	complex fraction
latitude	longitude	mean
pi	palindrome	ratio
square root	transversal	bit

PRODUCING PATTERNS

Write a number pattern on the board. Let students decide the pattern of that particular group of numbers:

Example:

2 4 6 8 10	**Pattern: increase by 2**
1 3 2 4 3 5 4	**Pattern: increase by 2, decrease by 1**
1 2 4 8 16 32	**Pattern: double each number**
5 10 15 20 25 30	**Pattern: consecutive multiples of 5**
25 24 20 19 15 14 10	**Pattern: decrease by 1, decrease by 4**

TWELVE QUESTIONS

Select a number from 1 to 100. Write it on a slip of paper so that you can show it to your students later.

Let students ask questions that you can answer with "yes" or "no." Their goal is to discover your number in twelve questions or less. You may want to count only those questions that result in a "no" response.

After a few rounds of questions, discuss the types of questions that help narrow down the choice of numbers:

✦ **Is it an even number?**

✦ **Is it greater than 50? Less than 50?**

✦ **Is the first digit larger than the second digit (if it is a two-digit number)?**

BONKERS

Ask your students to count aloud by ones as you go around the room. Before you start, select a set of multiples (example: multiples of 3).

Whenever a student's turn lands on a multiple of the selected number, the student says "Bonkers!" instead of the number. Encourage the students to go as quickly as they can.

Example:
All multiples of 3 are "Bonkers." Students count as follows: 1, 2, Bonkers, 4, 5, Bonkers, 7, 8, Bonkers, and so on.

To increase the complexity (and the fun), select two numbers whose multiples are to be "Bonkers" at the same time (for instance, 3 and 4).

PLACE IT

Have students draw 3 or 4 lines on a sheet of paper to be used as blank spaces. (Everyone should have the same number of blank lines.) Then call out a corresponding number of digits, one at a time. As you call out each one, the students should write it on one of their spaces in any order they choose. When you have finished calling out all the digits, ask students to share the numbers they constructed. List these combinations on the board. What is the largest number possible? The smallest number possible? What numbers could be made that fall between the largest and smallest?

To change this activity a little bit, tell students to try to make the largest (or smallest) number possible. However, chance is part of this activity. Students may not change the position of a digit once it is written on their papers.

(The students will consider it more fair if you write the digits 0 to 9 on cards and pull them at random.)

FACTOR FRENZY

Separate the class into two teams.

Call out a number. Let the teams alternate naming a factor of that number. The last team to name a factor scores a point. The other team answers first on the next number. Continue until one team has 10 points.

If your students are really good at finding factors, try a more difficult activity. Write two numbers (between 0 and 12) on the board. Have students name numbers that have both of those numbers as factors.

Example:
2 and 9 are the numbers you name.
18, 36, 54, 72 are all numbers that have both 2 and 9 as factors.

WORTHY WORDS

List the letters of the alphabet on the board with a number value for each (A = 1, B = 2, C = 3 . . . Z = 26).

Ask students:
+ **to make up words with a certain value (a value of 7: BAD, BE, DAB).**
+ **to calculate the total value of a certain word (ARITHMETIC = 106).**
+ **to calculate the value of their own names.**
+ **If letters cost the same as their point values (A = 1 cent), what words could they buy for a nickel? A dime? A quarter? A dollar?**
+ **If they can make a sentence using only nickel words, what would those words be?**

STATE THE PROBLEM

Give students an answer. Let them give you as many problems as possible to "fit" the answer.

You can complicate the activity by requiring that the problems involve a specific operation (addition, subtraction, multiplication, or division).

If you have a longer period of time, separate the class into two teams. Call out the answer. Then alternate between the two teams, letting each give you problems for that answer. If a team cannot think of another problem, the other team scores a point and gives the first response to the next answer.

TELL HOW

State a math task. Let students tell you how to accomplish it.

Examples:
- ✦ **Find the area of a square. (Multiply the length of a side by itself and express in square units.)**
- ✦ **Convert minutes to seconds. (Multiply by 60.)**
- ✦ **Find the perimeter of a figure. (Add all the sides.)**
- ✦ **Find the circumference of a cylinder when the diameter is known. (Multiply the diameter by 3.14.)**
- ✦ **Find an equivalent fraction for a given fraction. (Multiply the denominator and the numerator by the same number.)**
- ✦ **Convert feet to inches. (Multiply by 12.)**
- ✦ **Convert quarters to dollars. (Divide by 4.)**

IT'S A BARGAIN

Anytime that you can purchase a quality item below the normal price, it's a bargain. Some sales that are supposed to be great bargains really aren't.

Let your students decide which of the following sale prices are really bargains:

- ✦ **Candy bars 40¢ each**   **Sale 3/$1.00 (Bargain)**
- ✦ **Wacky shoelaces 75¢ a pair**   **Sale 2 pairs/$1.00 (Bargain)**
- ✦ **Pencils 10¢ each**   **Sale 3/25¢ (Bargain)**
- ✦ **Comic books 50¢ each**   **Sale 6/$3.50 (Not a bargain)**

Add other items to the list as you repeat this activity.

MONEY OFF

Many times sale prices are not directly listed. Instead, the ticket or sign will indicate an amount to be taken off the normal price.

Let the students practice computing the sale price when you give the normal price and the amount to be taken off. To really sharpen their skills, practice this activity two or three times a week for a few minutes at a time using different amounts.

Jeans $18.00	**½ off ($9.00)**
Shoes $25.00	**⅕ off ($20.00)**
Video game $20.00	**¼ off ($15.00)**
Gold chain $40.00	**½ off ($20.00)**
Record album $9.00	**⅓ off ($6.00)**
Board game $12.00	**⅙ off ($10.00)**

PROFIT OR LOSS?

Let students do some mental arithmetic as they try to determine whether a profit or a loss was realized on each of the following transactions:

1. **You bought 8 oranges for 10¢ each and sold them 8 for $1.00. (Profit)**
2. **You bought a bike for $59.00, added a new tire to it for $10.00, then sold it for $75.00. (Profit)**
3. **You bought 3 books at a garage sale for a total of $2.00. Later you sold one to your brother for 75¢. Then you sold the others to your best friend for 50¢ each. (Loss)**
4. **You spent $5.50 to buy seeds, fertilizer, and flower pots. Only 3 pots of marigolds actually grew. You sold each pot of flowers for $1.50. (Loss)**

Let your students bring in profit or loss problems for the class to solve.

Social Studies

Social Studies

Social Studies

Social Studies

Social Studies

Social Studies

Social Studies

Social Studies

Social Studies

Social Studies

WESTWARD HO!

List the following modes of transportation on the board. Let students help you put them in chronological order. Discuss how each mode has contributed to the development of this country.

steamboat	**automobile**
airplane	**space shuttle**
train	**canoe**
covered wagon	**horse**

What types of transportation do your students think might contribute to the future exploration of this country and of outer space?

COMMUNICATIONS

Students will name spoken and written language as our main means of communication, yet we share our thoughts, feelings, and values in many other ways. See if your students can think of other ways in which we communicate.

Examples:
  music
  clothing styles
  dance
  paintings, sculptures, and other art forms
  religious ceremonies
  plays, television, movies

LOOK AT THE USA

Let students open their social studies books to a map of the United States. Use this activity to give them practice finding features and places on the map.

- ✦ **Find our state.**
- ✦ **Name and locate a major chain of mountains.**
- ✦ **Name and locate at least two lakes and rivers.**
- ✦ **Name and locate some islands.**
- ✦ **Name and locate a peninsula.**
- ✦ **Find and name all the states that border our state.**

List additional activities on the back of this card for future use.

BOUNTIFUL RESOURCES

Our country is blessed with many rich resources.

List the letters of the alphabet down the side of the chalkboard and let students try to name a resource that starts with each letter.

Example:
   A = Apple orchards
   B = Birds
   C = Coal
   D = Deer

Try to name only natural items. Do not include artificial products.

SIGHTS TO SEE

Historic landmarks can be found all across the United States. Name some of the following sites. Ask if any student in your class has seen them. Let any student that has visited the site tell the class about it for a minute.

- ✦ **Mount Rushmore located in South Dakota (four presidents carved on the side of the mountain: Washington, Jefferson, Lincoln, T. Roosevelt)**
- ✦ **Statue of Liberty located in New York Harbor**
- ✦ **The Lincoln Memorial located in Washington, D.C.**
- ✦ **The Tomb of the Unknown Soldier located in Arlington, Virginia**
- ✦ **The Liberty Bell located in Philadelphia**

What other historic landmarks have your students visited or read about?

NAME ANOTHER

Instruct your students to open their social studies books to a map of an area that they have studied.

Name a particular item by its proper name. Then ask the students to name another of the same item.

Example: (Looking at the USA map: Teacher, "Rio Grande River." Students, "Hudson River.")

You may want to name:

rivers	**cities**	**highways**
mountain ranges	**lakes**	**countries**
states	**oceans**	**continents**

AD-VICE

Divide your class into four teams. Assign each team a different advertising medium: radio, TV, newspapers, or billboards. Announce that you have just created a wonderful new candy. You are willing to spend all your advertising budget on one type of advertising.

Let the teams brainstorm for two minutes to think of as many reasons as possible why your candy should be advertised through their medium. They may also list disadvantages of the other advertising methods.

Give each team one minute to share their reasons with the class. Then have the students vote for the type of advertising that makes the most sense for the product. Don't let students vote for their own advertising.

Repeat this activity another time using a different product.

IN DEMAND

Remind students how the law of supply and demand works:
When demand is high, supply decreases and value increases.
When demand is low, supply increases and value decreases.

Ask students to name examples of this law based on their own experiences. How many of them were unable to purchase a particular compact disc that was on the top ten list when they wanted it?

Other Examples:
During the Christmas season, certain toys are in great demand. The latest video games, new dolls, and certain styles of clothing and shoes are hard to find. Later when their popularity fades, these items are sold at drastically reduced prices.

JOBS! JOBS! JOBS!

New products mean more jobs. Have your students trace the production of one of these products from beginning to end, naming all of the jobs that are associated with its production and its distribution to consumers.

a pair of tennis shoes	soft drink
automobile	textbook
bicycle	a pair of eyeglasses
a pair of designer jeans	greeting card
candy bar	Christmas tree
movie	pencil

BEST FOOT FORWARD

Discuss competition for jobs. A good example is the number of teenagers applying for summer jobs at fast food restaurants. Let students share their ideas of how job applicants can "put their best foot forward" when applying for a job. Some ideas to consider:

✦ attention to personal hygiene

✦ manner of speaking

✦ appropriate clothing

✦ handwriting and spelling on application form

✦ confidence and poise during interview

✦ interest in job responsibilities

✦ presentation of previous experience

✦ letters of recommendation

WORTHY WORKERS

Compensation is not always commensurate with the services provided by workers. List or name the following jobs and services. Ask students to rank them according to the amount they should be paid (from lowest to highest salary):

teacher   secretary
law enforcement officer   doctor
garbage collector   author
professional athlete   bus driver
firefighter   rock musician

Let students discuss why they ranked the jobs as they did.

CONTINENTAL QUIZ

To help students become more familiar with the continents and to give them an opportunity to use globes, ask them these questions. If you have globes, let groups of students look at them for three to five minutes while you ask:

✦ **Does the equator pass through Africa?**
✦ **Why could we call Europe and Asia Eurasia?**
✦ **Are North and South America connected by land?**
✦ **Is Antarctica north of Europe?**
✦ **Are Africa and Australia connected by land?**

Let students ask questions of the rest of the class.

BRAIN POWER

Remind students that most jobs have certain skill or knowledge requirements. Some jobs require more education than others.

Let students name specific jobs that fit into the following educational requirement categories:

- ✦ **no education at all**
- ✦ **less than high-school diploma**
- ✦ **high-school diploma**
- ✦ **college degree**
- ✦ **specialized training (may or may not include a college education)**

CONSUMER OR PRODUCER

Our country enjoys a free enterprise system. People who make things are called producers. People who buy and use things are called consumers. Let your students tell which they would be if they:

- ✦ **bought a transformer toy at the mall.**
- ✦ **made french fries at a fast food restaurant.**
- ✦ **operated a lemonade stand in your neighborhood.**
- ✦ **bought a movie ticket.**
- ✦ **went to the barbershop for a haircut.**
- ✦ **created original Christmas cards for friends.**
- ✦ **purchased new school supplies.**

THOUGHTS OF FREEDOM

Discuss the Statue of Liberty and its history. Call on individual students to explain what the word "freedom" means to them.

Ask your students to distinguish between small and large freedoms as you call on different students to finish the sentence, "Freedom is to be able to . . ."

Examples:
- ✦ . . . vote on election day.
- ✦ . . . choose what kind of sandwich I want for lunch.
- ✦ . . . spend my own money on whatever I want.
- ✦ . . . decide what kind of job I want.

RESOURCE DILEMMA

We are constantly making choices about the use of our natural resources. Students should be aware of the variety of ways in which we can use our resources. As adults they will be making decisions that will affect future generations.

Ask students to name ways that each of the following resources could be used and to decide which uses are most important or appropriate.

- ✦ **A river: to harness for electricity, to use for transportation, to use for recreational activities, to fish commercially**
- ✦ **An uninhabited piece of land: to use as a park, to build houses, to set aside as a nature preserve, to build a parking lot, to zone for commercial buildings**
- ✦ **A large area of timberland: to cut trees for lumber, to partially clear for a park, to cut trees for houses, to leave as a natural preserve**

JUMBLED STATES

Give your students one of the jumbled state names listed below and let
them "unjumble" it. You might want to keep track of their record times.

Alabama — Balmaaa
Alaska — Sklaaa
Arizona — Ziranoa
Arkansas — Ssaaknra
California — Aafciirnol
Colorado — Acdlooor
Connecticut — Nccoienttuc
Delaware — Adaeelrw
Florida — Afdirlo
Georgia — Aeiggor
Hawaii — Aaihwi
Idaho — Adioh
Illinois — Siiillno
Indiana — Aadiinn
Iowa — Aiow
Kansas — Aakssn

Kentucky — Centkkuy
Louisiana — Aaiiousnl
Maine — Aeinm
Maryland — Aadlnmry
Massachusetts — Acaesstthumss
Michigan — Achigmni
Minnesota — Aeimnostn
Mississippi — Iiippssssm
Missouri — Iissrmou
Montana — Aantomn
Nebraska — Aaebksrn
Nevada — Aadenv
New Hampshire — Aeeihpnwmsrh
New Jersey — Eeewrjsyn
New Mexico — Eecionmwx
New York — Eoykrwn
North Carolina — Aaionorthcrln

North Dakota — Aaootkdthrn
Ohio — Iooh
Oklahoma — Aaooklhm
Oregon — Ooegnr
Pennsylvania — Aaiennspylvn
Rhode Island — Aioedhrsndl
South Carolina — Aaoouicsthrln
South Dakota — Aauootkdhts
Tennessee — Eeeessnnt
Texas — Aetsx
Utah — Ahut
Vermont — Eotnmrv
Virginia — Aiingrvi
Washington — Aiontgnhsw
West Virginia — Estwaiiingrv
Wisconsin — Iiowscnsn
Wyoming — Gioynmw

CAPITAL CATCH

Call out the name of a state in the USA, and ask the students to name the state's capital.
Play this game at least once a week until students learn all of the states and their capitals.

Alabama—Montgomery
Alaska—Juneau
Arizona—Phoenix
Arkansas—Little Rock
California—Sacramento
Colorado—Denver
Connecticut—Hartford
Delaware—Dover
Florida—Tallahassee
Georgia—Atlanta
Hawaii—Honolulu
Idaho—Boise
Illinois—Springfield
Indiana—Indianapolis
Iowa—Des Moines
Kansas—Topeka

Kentucky—Frankfort
Louisiana—Baton Rouge
Maine—Augusta
Maryland—Annapolis
Massachusetts—Boston
Michigan—Lansing
Minnesota—St. Paul
Mississippi—Jackson
Missouri—Jefferson City
Montana—Helena
Nebraska—Lincoln
Nevada—Carson City
New Hampshire—Concord
New Jersey—Trenton
New Mexico—Santa Fe
New York—Albany
North Carolina—Raleigh

North Dakota—Bismark
Ohio—Columbus
Oklahoma—Oklahoma City
Oregon—Salem
Pennsylvania—Harrisburg
Rhode Island—Providence
South Carolina—Columbia
South Dakota—Pierre
Tennessee—Nashville
Texas—Austin
Utah—Salt Lake City
Vermont—Montpelier
Virginia—Richmond
Washington—Olympia
West Virginia—Charleston
Wisconsin—Madison
Wyoming—Cheyenne

NATIVE AMERICAN KNOW-HOW

The first Americans made many valuable contributions to our country. List three headings on the board:

food and plants   **medicines**   **inventions**

Explain that the following are contributions made by Native Americans. Ask students to tell which heading each contribution belongs under:

pipe	cotton	moccasins
dog sled	squash	pumpkin
corn	quinine	hammock
witch hazel	petroleum jelly	popcorn
peanuts	canoe	

Can your students add other Native American contributions to the list?

INVENTION MATCH

Name a famous inventor and ask the students to name the correct invention. Or, name the invention and let the students name the inventor responsible.

✦ **Benjamin Franklin** ....lightning rod

✦ **Alexander Graham Bell** ....telephone

✦ **Samuel Morse** ....telegraph

✦ **Wright Brothers** ....first successful airplane

✦ **Clarence Birdseye**...................................frozen food process

✦ **Thomas Edison** ....light bulb, phonograph

✦ **Elisha Graves Otis** ....elevator

✦ **Jonas Salk** ....polio vaccine

OLDER OR BETTER?

Most products are worth more when they are new than when they are old, but that is not true of all items. Some products increase in value if they are kept a long time (especially if they remain in good condition).

Have students name items that they think will increase in value if they are kept for a long time. This list will help you get started:

well-made furniture
paintings by famous artists
comic books
rare books/first editions
baseball cards
newspaper editions with significant historical headlines
cosmetic bottles
letters from famous people

TIME MACHINE

Tell your students to pretend that they can climb into a time machine and go backward or forward in time. They will always land in the same place, just in a different time. Let them take turns describing their trips into the past or the future. Ask:

✦ **What does the area look like?**

✦ **How are the people dressed?**

✦ **What work do you see people doing?**

✦ **How are people traveling during this time?**

✦ **What do you notice that is most different from present time?**

Use this activity once a week and allow the students to research the time to which they want to travel.

POLLUTION PATROL

Encourage your students to be aware of local litter and pollution problems. Ask them to name some of the local recreational areas and to think about the kinds of litter they have seen in those places.

What can you do at the local level to stop pollution of your community environment? Discuss community programs that are aimed at curbing litter and pollution.

What is being done at your school to stop littering? Ask your students to look out for litter they see as they move around the school campus. Are there ways they can help? Can you make posters? Do trash cans need to be put in more spots? Discuss what your class can do.

PEACE LINKS

Our students will be responsible for world peace in the future. Discuss these questions with them for a few minutes:

- ✦ **Why do you think peace is important?**
- ✦ **Why do you think peace is difficult to achieve?**
- ✦ **How can you begin to prepare for your role in the future of world peace? (Discuss the importance of learning about other countries and their people.)**
- ✦ **What can we do now to help us learn about other parts of the world?**

WHAT IS IT?

Use this quiz to help students practice map and globe skills. Ask volunteers to define each of the terms listed below:

Key: tells what the symbols on a map represent

Legend: tells what the symbols on a map represent

Scale: tells what each measured unit of distance on the map stands for in real distance

Longitude: imaginary lines that run east and west on the earth's surface

Latitude: imaginary lines that run north and south on the earth's surface

Equator: imaginary line that runs around the center of the earth, separating the north and south hemispheres

LEGENDARY LEARNING

Let your students imagine they are going to make a map of their city. Give them the following words and let them volunteer to come to the board and draw a symbol for that object as if it were going to be used on the map legend.

If you have a longer period of time, let each student make a complete set of symbols for a legend on his or her own paper.

tree	day-care center
school building	sports field
house	restaurant
playground	airport
store	library
office building	grocery store

IT'S CUSTOMARY

Every country in the world has unique social customs. The United States has many customs that we might not even think about; they are a part of our everyday life. Ask your students to think of customs practiced in this country that might be done differently in other parts of the world.

Here are some to get them started:

+ **shaking hands when meeting someone**
+ **sending greeting cards at Christmas**
+ **families eating meals together**
+ **pledging allegiance to the flag in school each day**
+ **filling baskets with colored eggs for Easter**

UNIVERSAL SIGNS

We don't always have to speak the same language in order to communicate with people from other lands. There are many gestures and expressions that mean the same thing to all people. How many can your students name?

+ **beckoning with a finger**

+ **holding palm upright to mean "stop"**

+ **putting one's finger to his or her lips to command silence**

+ **shrugging shoulders to indicate puzzlement or uncertainty**

+ **waving good-bye**

+ **scratching one's head to indicate confusion or uncertainty**

WEATHER WORRIES

Weather and climate play an important role in the way people live in various parts of the world. Discuss the difference between weather and climate.

Weather: the particular atmospheric conditions at any given time in a specific place

Climate: the overall year-round weather patterns of a particular place

Discuss:
- ✦ **What would happen if the earth's temperature began to increase constantly?**
- ✦ **What would happen if the amount of precipitation suddenly decreased?**
- ✦ **What would happen if we no longer had changes of seasons?**

BE RESOURCEFUL

Our natural resources are invaluable to us. Many resources are in limited supply. We must use our resources carefully.

Name one of the resources listed below and let the students discuss ways it might be used. Encourage them to discuss problems that might occur from overuse or abuse of each resource. Which uses are most appropriate? What conflicts arise when choices have to be made? How should these decisions be made? Who controls each resource?
- ✦ **forest area**
- ✦ **natural gas**
- ✦ **ocean beach**
- ✦ **fossil fuels**
- ✦ **large rivers (such as the Mississippi)**

STATES IN JEOPARDY

Ask the students to open their social studies books to a map of the United States. Using the Jeopardy game format, give the students an answer and let them call out the appropriate question.

Examples:

✦ **This state is a peninsula. (What is Florida, Alaska?)**

✦ **These states' borders form right angles where they meet. (What are Utah, Colorado, Arizona, and New Mexico?)**

✦ **This state has the Rio Grande River as a border with a foreign country. (What is Texas?)**

Make up more answers based on the social studies map available to you.

OLD GLORY

Discuss the pledge of allegiance to the flag with your students. Ask students to define each of these words:

✦ **pledge: a promise**

✦ **allegiance: loyalty**

✦ **indivisible: unable to be divided**

Find out what your students know about "Old Glory":

✦ **What do the stars represent?**

✦ **How many stars are there?**

✦ **How many stripes are there?**

✦ **What do the stripes represent?**

COMMUNITY HELPERS

Ask the students to name various community helpers that provide goods or services for them. Select one from the list they name and discuss the consequences if that person were no longer available.

Some helpers students might name include:
- ✦ **doctors**
- ✦ **teachers**
- ✦ **mail delivery persons**
- ✦ **garbage collectors**
- ✦ **firefighters**
- ✦ **weather reporters (meteorologists)**
- ✦ **ministers, priests, rabbis**

I NEED, I WANT

Discuss with your class the basic needs of human beings. Use this activity to give them practice discriminating between needs and wants.

As you name each item let students respond with "need" or "want." (If your students are restless, let them stand up for "needs" and sit down for "wants."

shelter	**shoes**	**electric heater**
ice-cream soda	**stereo**	**soap**
bathing suit	**socks**	**underwear**
visit to the doctor	**candy bar**	**tennis lessons**
trip to the amusement park	**milk**	**sleeping bag**
new toy	**bed**	**fresh air**
haircut	**tape recorder**	**water**

LITTER TELLS!

Archeologists learn much by studying the remains of ancient civilizations. What will future archeologists learn about us by examining our litter? What kinds of things will they find when they dig up our ruins thousands of years from now?

Let your students make a list of the things that they think are characteristic of our society at the present time.

Some starters:

tennis shoes	**computer**	**footballs**
soft drink cans	**joysticks**	**televisions**
curling irons	**skateboards**	**compact discs**

MI CASA, SU CASA

Having a home or a shelter is a basic need of humans. Ask students to tell who might live in the following houses or shelters:

- ✦ **adobe hut**
- ✦ **igloo**
- ✦ **barrack**
- ✦ **dormitory**
- ✦ **mansion**
- ✦ **tent**
- ✦ **The White House**
- ✦ **palace**

ROBOT RIOT

Discuss what computers do now and what they may do in the future. Do you think they will be able to do many of the little things we do for ourselves now?

Let students decide how robots or computers could be involved with some of the following daily activities. Would you want robots to do all of these things for you?

- ✦ **getting out of bed in the morning (robot pulls back covers, etc.)**
- ✦ **getting dressed for work or school**
- ✦ **brushing teeth, combing hair**
- ✦ **preparing meals**
- ✦ **doing homework, writing reports**
- ✦ **doing household chores, yard work**

DAYS TO CELEBRATE

The significance of patriotic holidays often becomes obscured. Give the name of one of the following holidays or the special date. Let students tell why that date is a holiday. Why do we celebrate that date? Be sure to point out that some holidays have been changed by the federal government to fall on a Monday as a matter of convenience.

Lincoln's Birthday	**February 12th**
Washington's Birthday	**February 22nd**
Memorial Day	**May 30th**
Flag Day	**June 14th**
Independence Day	**July 4th**
Columbus Day	**October 12th**
Veterans Day	**November 11th**
Thanksgiving	**4th Thursday of November**

CHANGING TIMES

Modern life is very different from life a long time ago. As a class, list things about our way of life that have changed:

Since the students were born

cable TV	**common use of**	**heart transplants**
shuttle trips into	**computers**	**compact discs**
outer space	**velcro fasteners**	

Since their grandparents were born

television	**space travel**	**microwave ovens**
bionic parts for	**freeze-dried**	
humans	**foods**	

Self-Awareness

Self-Awareness

Self-Awareness

Self-Awareness

Self-Awareness

Self-Awareness

Self-Awareness

Self-Awareness

Self-Awareness

Self-Awareness

VALUE JUDGMENTS

Lead the class in a discussion of one of the following value questions:

- ✦ **Can you ever be too nice to someone?**
- ✦ **Are there ever times when you shouldn't tell the truth?**
- ✦ **Is it always best to keep a secret?**
- ✦ **When would it be okay to break a promise?**
- ✦ **When would it be okay to disobey an adult?**

NOT RIGHT NOW!

Everyone has situations or events that they would like to avoid or postpone. That is why so many people are procrastinators.

Ask each student to tell something that he or she would rather not do "right" now.

Some examples might be:

- ✦ **face parents with a poor report card**
- ✦ **complete a spelling assignment**
- ✦ **take a test**
- ✦ **wash dishes**
- ✦ **start a diet**

FINISH IT

Ask the students to respond to one of the following open-ended statements, and watch them discover their own feelings.

+ **I feel happiest when . . .**
+ **I'm a good friend because . . .**
+ **The best thing that ever happened to me was . . .**
+ **Nothing makes me angrier than . . .**
+ **I'm really afraid of . . .**
+ **Someday I want to . . .**
+ **I can't stand people who . . .**

SHOW YOU CARE

Many times young adults want to show others that they care about them, but they don't know the appropriate thing to do in some circumstances.

Ask your students to discuss what might be done to show how much they care in the following situations:

+ **A friend is very unhappy over his or her parents' divorce or remarriage.**
+ **Your best friend's pet died.**
+ **Someone you love has a serious illness.**
+ **Someone just did something embarrassing in front of other people.**
+ **Your classmate's sister was killed in an automobile accident.**

I'M IN CHARGE

Young adults often feel that they never get to be in charge of anything; someone else is always in charge of them. Let them discuss what they would do if they were in charge of . . .

- ✦ **the school (Ask for serious responses.)**
- ✦ **their families (Would they change their family rules, etc.?)**
- ✦ **our country (What laws would they create or abolish?)**
- ✦ **the entire world (What could they do to promote peace?)**

UNDER PRESSURE

Students of all ages experience peer pressure. Help your students learn to deal with such situations by doing some role-playing in your classroom.

Select two students. One student will put pressure on the other one to do something that isn't quite right. The other student will try to resist the pressure without ruining the friendship. The "pressuring" friend might say:

- ✦ **Could I copy your homework? I forgot mine.**
- ✦ **Let's try this cigarette that I found in the bathroom.**
- ✦ **While I distract the clerk, you grab a couple of candy bars.**
- ✦ **Let's take that five-dollar bill that your mom left on the table.**
- ✦ **How about skipping school with me today? No one will know.**

GOOD DEEDS

There is a saying that the best things in life are free.

Ask your students to name some of the nice things that they can do for others without spending money. If you have time, make a list of the good deeds they name and post it as a reminder to everyone.

Some free good deeds:
- ✦ **Compliment a person on something he or she has done.**
- ✦ **Share something of yours with someone else.**
- ✦ **Listen to a friend's trouble.**
- ✦ **Offer to help with a problem or chore.**
- ✦ **Spend time with someone who is lonely.**
- ✦ **Introduce two of your friends to each other.**

THE GOOD AND THE BAD

Most students grumble and complain about school. This activity stimulates them to think about what they like about school as well as what they dislike.

Make two lists on the board under the headings "good" and "bad." Let the students take turns. If the first student names something to go under the "bad" list, then the next student must name something to be placed in the "good" list.

Some possible good things: place to see my old friends and meet new ones, it would be boring to be home all of the time, learn new things, etc.

Some possible bad things: too much work, can't talk enough, don't like the lunches, would rather be outside or watching TV, etc.

CHANGING ME

Ask each student to name something about him- or herself that has changed:

+ **in the past twenty-four hours (clothing, hair style, mood)**
+ **in the past seven days (age, weight, something learned to do)**
+ **in the past year (joined Scouts, changed grades, broke leg)**
+ **since birth (almost anything will fit here)**

Ask students to predict what changes they will experience in the next year . . . five years . . . ten years.

MY DREAM ROOM

Ask students to describe their dream classrooms by responding to these questions:

+ **What color would the walls in your dream classroom be?**
+ **What kind of furniture would be in it?**
+ **How would the furniture be arranged?**
+ **Would there be anything unusual about this room?**
+ **Would your dream classroom have windows?**
+ **What kind of desk would the teacher have?**
+ **How would your dream classroom differ from your present classroom?**

ONE TO TEN

Have your students mentally rate themselves on a scale of 1 to 10 in relationship to these qualities or situations (1 is a poor rating and 10 is a high rating):

✦ I am a loyal friend.

✦ I am good at taking tests.

✦ I get along with other people.

✦ I can entertain myself.

✦ I am an athlete.

✦ I am cheerful.

✦ I practice good health habits.

✦ I control my temper.

✦ I am a positive influence on my peers.

A FRIEND IS . . .

Ask students: "Who knows what a friend is?"

Probably all of the students will raise their hands. Call on students one at a time to complete this sentence: "A friend is someone who . . . ."

If you have more time, post a long piece of craft paper on the bulletin board and let each student write and illustrate his or her version of "A friend is . . . ."

NAME GAME

Have one student come to the front of the room and write his or her name in large letters vertically down one side of the chalkboard.

Then let the rest of the class write a name poem for that student by writing a descriptive word that begins with each letter of the name. Emphasize personal qualities rather than physical appearance.

Examples:

Merry	**Jolly**	**Lovely**
Artistic	**Outgoing**	**Eager**
Restful	**Enthusiastic**	**Sensitive**
Talented		**Lively**
Aware		**Intelligent**
		Even-tempered

EXPRESS IT

Ask students to use sounds and body language to express how they would feel if in one of these situations:

- **Tomorrow is the day of the big field trip at school, and you just broke out in measles today.**
- **Your birthday present is exactly what you asked for!**
- **You are almost asleep, and you hear a strange noise in your closet.**
- **You lose sight of your parents at the airport fifteen minutes before your plane is scheduled to take off.**
- **You are trying to watch a concert, and everyone in front of you is taller than you are.**
- **You are last in the lunch line, and the cafeteria has run out of brownies.**

MIRROR, MIRROR

Young adults need an opportunity to look closely at themselves. Give each student or pair of students a small hand mirror and these instructions:

- **Look closely at yourself in the mirror.**

- **While you look, describe yourself to a friend. What color are your eyes? What shape are your eyes? What shape is your mouth? Are your ears attached to your head all the way down or does your earlobe hang free at the end? Do you have freckles? Is your skin dark or light? Follow the shape of your hairline in the front. Does it look the same all the way across, or does it peak in the front?**

- **Place the mirror so that you can see only half of your face at a time. Do both halves look the same? If not, what is different about the halves?**

A BETTER ME

Discuss the idea of self-improvement with your class. Point out that no one is perfect; there is something about each one of us that could be improved.

Give each student the opportunity to name something about him- or herself that could be improved. Remind the class that each person needs to be able to do this activity without anyone else making the participant feel uncomfortable or embarrassed.

If you will first name something about yourself that you want to improve, it will then be easier for students to evaluate themselves.

INDEPENDENCE DAY

By the time students are in the intermediate grades, they may have daydreamed about living on their own. They usually think only of the freedom that they would have. They very seldom consider the cost of providing for themselves.

As a class activity, have the students try to list all the goods and services they would have to pay for if they were living on their own.

They will name the obvious items (rent, groceries, telephone service). Try to guide them into discussion of the seemingly little items, like toothpaste and garbage collection fee, that they may skip.

TO KNOW ME . . .

Let each student quickly draw a picture of him- or herself. Then ask them to pass the papers around the room for a minute or so to make sure that no one has his or her own drawing.

Let each student try to match up the drawing he or she has with the correct artist.

If you have more time, post the pictures and number them. Let everyone make a list of the numbers and write the name of the correct student next to each one. Go over the list so that students can find out how many pictures they guessed correctly.

MOVE TO THIS SIDE

Find out how your students are alike and different. Have all of the students stand on one side of the room. Then say, "Move to this side if . . . ." Finish your statement with one of the choices listed below. Students move from side to side to indicate their preferences.

"Move to this side (indicate side) if you'd rather . . ."

- . . . **wear yellow than blue.**
- . . . **eat liver than spinach.**
- . . . **do reading homework than math homework.**
- . . . **play soccer than watch TV.**
- . . . **eat pizza than hamburgers.**
- . . . **be spanked than grounded.**

IT'S ME

Ask each student to write a brief description of him- or herself. Have them pass the papers to you. Read aloud each description and see if the rest of the class can identify the student. (Be sure to include a description of yourself!)

This activity can be extended by assigning each paper a number. Post the descriptions on a bulletin board. Let each student number a paper to match the numbers on the descriptions. Then, throughout the day or over a period of several days, students can list the students' names next to the numbers they think match the descriptions. Identify the correct names to let each student see how many he or she guessed correctly.

SHARE YOURS

Pass an object around the room from student to student. Whenever you say, "Stop," the student holding the object must share his or her answer to one of these questions:

- **"What is your best school subject?"**
- **"What color makes you feel happy? sad?"**
- **"What famous person would you like to be like?"**
- **"If you could have a different name, what would it be?"**
- **"If I could grant you one wish, what would it be?"**
- **"If you had to be one age forever, what age would you be?"**
- **"If you could make one change in your school, what would it be?"**

INDEX

INDEX